D1139055

Titles in Series S892

Little Tommy Tucker and other nursery rhymes

Little Jack Horner and other nursery rhymes

Little Bo Peep and other nursery rhymes

Little Miss Muffet and other nursery rhymes

British Library Cataloguing in Publication Data

Little Bo Peep and other nursery rhymes.
 I. Bracken, Carolyn
 398'.8
  ISBN 0-7214-9592-3

First edition

Published by Ladybird Books Ltd Loughborough Leicestershire UK
Ladybird Books Inc Auburn Maine 04210 USA

© LADYBIRD BOOKS LTD MCMLXXXIX
All rights reserved. No part of this publication may be reproduced, stored in a retrieval system, or transmitted in any form or by any means,
electronic, mechanical, photo-copying, recording or otherwise, without the prior consent of the copyright owner.

Printed in England

Little Bo Peep

and other nursery rhymes

Illustrated by Carolyn Bracken

Ladybird Books

Little Bo Peep has lost her sheep,
And doesn't know where to find them.
Leave them alone and they'll come home,
Wagging their tails behind them.

See-saw, Margery Daw,
Johnny shall have a new master;
He shall have but a penny a day,
Because he can't work any faster.

Higgledy Piggledy, my black hen,
She lays eggs for gentlemen;
Sometimes nine,
And sometimes ten,
Higgledy Piggledy, my black hen.

Little Boy Blue, come blow your horn,
The sheep's in the meadow, the cow's in the corn.
Where is the boy who looks after the sheep?
He's under the haystack, fast asleep.
Will you wake him? No, not I!
For if I do, he's sure to cry.

Hush, little baby, don't say a word,
Papa's going to buy you a mockingbird.
If that mockingbird won't sing,

Papa's going to buy you a diamond ring.
If that diamond ring turns to brass,

Papa's going to buy you a looking glass.
If that looking glass gets broke,

Papa's going to buy you a billy goat.
If that billy goat won't pull,

Papa's going to buy you a cart and bull.
If that cart and bull fall down,

You'll still be the sweetest little baby in town!

Pat-a-cake, pat-a-cake, baker's man,
Bake me a cake as fast as you can;
Pat it and prick it, and mark it with B,
And put it in the oven for Baby and me.

Andy Pandy, fine and dandy,
Loves plum cake and sugar candy.
Bought it from a candy shop,
And away did hop, hop, hop.

The Queen of Hearts she made some tarts,
All on a summer's day;
The Knave of Hearts he stole those tarts,
And took them clean away.
The King of Hearts called for the tarts,
And beat the Knave full sore;
The Knave of Hearts brought
                         back the tarts,
And vowed he'd steal no more.

There was an old woman lived under a hill,
And if she's not gone, she lives there still.
Baked apples she sold, and cranberry pies,
And she's the old woman who never told lies.

There was an old woman who lived in a shoe;
She had so many children she didn't know what to do;
She gave them some broth without any bread,
And whipped them all soundly and sent them to bed.

Péter Piper picked a peck of pickled peppers;
A peck of pickled peppers Peter Piper picked.

If Peter Piper picked a peck of pickled peppers,
Where's the peck of pickled peppers Peter Piper picked?

A cat came fiddling out of a barn,
With a pair of bagpipes under her arm;
She could sing nothing but "Fiddle-de-dee,
The mouse has married the bumblebee."
Pipe, cat; dance, mouse;
We'll have a wedding at our good house.

Lavender's blue, dilly, dilly,
Lavender's green;
When I am king, dilly, dilly,
You shall be queen.

I saw three ships come sailing by,
Come sailing by, come sailing by,
I saw three ships come sailing by,
On Christmas Day in the morning.

And what do you think was in them then,
Was in them then, was in them then?
And what do you think was in them then,
On Christmas Day in the morning?

Three pretty girls were in them then,
Were in them then, were in them then,
Three pretty girls were in them then,
On Christmas Day in the morning.

One could whistle, and one could sing,
And one could play the violin;
Such joy there was at my wedding,
On Christmas Day in the morning.

I had a little nut tree,
Nothing would it bear
But a silver nutmeg
And a golden pear.

The King of Spain's daughter
Came to visit me,
And all for the sake
Of my little nut tree.

Ring-a-ring o' roses,
A pocket full of posies,
A-tishoo! A-tishoo!
We all fall down.

Sally go round the sun,
Sally go round the moon,
Sally go round the chimney pot
On a Saturday afternoon.

Rock-a-bye, baby, in the tree top,
When the wind blows, the cradle will rock;
When the bough breaks, the cradle will fall;
Down will come baby, cradle, and all.

Up and down the City Road,
In and out the Eagle,
That's the way the money goes,
Pop goes the weasel!

Half a pound of tuppenny rice,
Half a pound of treacle,
Mix it up and make it nice,
Pop goes the weasel!

Goosey, goosey, gander,
Where shall I wander?
Upstairs, downstairs,
In my lady's chamber.

Cackle, cackle, Mother Goose,
Have you any feathers loose?
Truly have I, pretty fellow,
Half enough to fill a pillow.

Here are quills,
    take one or two,
And down to make
    a bed for you.

Good night, sleep tight,
Wake up bright in the morning light,
To do what's right with all your might.